MERRY CHRISTMAS

1986
To my darling god
daughter, may god
Bless you Love
mom

FOR
PAUL

Copyright © MCMLXX by
The C. R. Gibson Company, Norwalk, Connecticut
All rights reserved
Printed in the United States of America
Library of Congress Catalog Card Number: 73-101450

ISBN 0-8378-2001-4

The wonderful
Promises of God
as expressed in the
TWENTY-THIRD PSALM
together with
other choice portions of
HOLY SCRIPTURE

COMPILED AND ILLUSTRATED
BY ROYAL V. CARLEY

The C. R. Gibson Company, *Publishers*
Norwalk, Connecticut

THE LORD: is my shepherd,
I shall not want.

SECURITY

Take no thought, saying, What shall we eat? or, What shall we drink? .... For your heavenly Father knoweth that ye have need of all these things. But seek ye first the kingdom of God, and his righteousness; and all these things shall be added unto you.

Matthew 6:31, 32, 33

He shall feed his flock like a shepherd: ...

Isaiah 40:11

The Lord is my light and my salvation; whom shall I fear? the Lord is the strength of my life; of whom shall I be afraid?

Psalm 27:1

The Lord shall preserve thy going out and thy coming in from this time forth, and even for evermore.

Psalm 121:8

I am the good shepherd: the good shepherd giveth his life for the sheep.

John 10:11

But my God shall supply all your need according to his riches in glory by Christ Jesus.

Philippians 4:19

He maketh me to lie down in green pastures...

HAPPINESS

We will rejoice in thy salvation, and in the name of our God we will set up our banners: the Lord fulfil all thy petitions.

Psalm 20:5

Know ye that the Lord he is God: it is he that hath made us, and not we ourselves; we are his people and the sheep of his pasture.

Psalm 100:3

Happy is he that hath the God of Jacob for his help, whose hope is in the Lord his God: . . .

Psalm 146:5

. . . . but rather rejoice, because your names are written in heaven.

Luke 10:20

But I have trusted in thy mercy; my heart shall rejoice in thy salvation.

Psalm 13:5

...he leadeth me beside the still waters.

PEACE

Thou wilt keep him in perfect peace, whose mind is stayed on thee: because he trusteth in thee.
Isaiah 26:3

Come unto me, all ye that labour and are heavy laden, and I will give you rest.
Matthew 11:28

But the fruit of the Spirit is love, joy, peace, . . .
Galatians 5:22

Be careful for nothing; but in every thing by prayer and supplication with thanksgiving let your requests be made known unto God. And the peace of God, which passeth all understanding, shall keep your hearts and minds through Christ Jesus.
Philippians 4:6, 7

Now the God of hope fill you with all joy and peace in believing, that ye may abound in hope, through the power of the Holy Ghost.
Romans 15:13

He restoreth my soul…

STRENGTH

The Lord is my strength and my
shield; my heart trusted in him,
and I am helped: therefore my
heart greatly rejoiceth; and with
my song will I praise him.

Psalm 28:7

. . . in quietness and in confidence
shall be your strength: . . .

Isaiah 30:15

. . . be strong in the Lord and in
the power of his might. Put on
the whole armour of God, that
ye may be able to stand against
the wiles of the devil.

Ephesians 6:10, 11

. . . for the joy of the Lord is
your strength.

Nehemiah 8:10

Now I know that the Lord saveth
his anointed; he will hear him
from his holy heaven with the
saving strength of his right
hand.

Psalm 20:6

But they that wait upon the Lord
shall renew their strength; they
shall mount up with wings as
eagles; they shall run, and not be
weary; and they shall walk, and
not faint.

Isaiah 40:31

...he leadeth me in the paths of righteousness for his name's sake.

GUIDANCE

The steps of a good man are ordered by the Lord: and he delighteth in his way.

Psalm 37:23

I will instruct thee and teach thee in the way which thou shalt go: I will guide thee with mine eye.

Psalm 32:8

Thy word is a lamp unto my feet, and a light unto my path.

Psalm 119:105

Then spake Jesus ... saying, I am the light of the world: he that followeth me shall not walk in darkness, but shall have the light of life.

John 8:12

And thine ears shall hear a word behind thee, saying, This is the way, walk ye in it, when ye turn to the right hand, and when ye turn to the left.

Isaiah 30:21

Yea, though I walk through the valley of the shadow of death, I will fear no evil...

ASSURANCE

...our Saviour, Jesus Christ, who hath abolished death, and hath brought life and immortality to light through the gospel: ...

II Timothy 1:10

But now is Christ risen from the dead, and become the firstfruits of them that slept.

I Corinthians 15:20

Wherefore he is able also to save them to the uttermost that come unto God by him, seeing he ever liveth to make intercession for them.

Hebrews 7:25

The last enemy that shall be destroyed is death.

I Corinthians 15:26

And God shall wipe away all tears from their eyes; and there shall be no more death, neither sorrow, nor crying, neither shall there be any more pain: for the former things are passed away.

Revelation 21:4

...for thou art with me; thy rod and thy staff they comfort me.

HIS PRESENCE

And the Lord, he it is that doth go before thee; he will be with thee, he will not fail thee, neither forsake thee: fear not, neither be dismayed.

Deuteronomy 31:8

... I will never leave thee, nor forsake thee. So that we may boldly say, The Lord is my helper, and I will not fear what man shall do unto me.

Hebrews 13:5, 6

The Lord is nigh unto them that are of broken heart; and saveth such as be of a contrite spirit.

Psalm 34:18

When thou passest through the waters, I will be with thee; and through the rivers, they shall not overflow thee: ...

Isaiah 43:2

Blessed be God, even the Father of our Lord Jesus Christ, the Father of mercies, and the God of all comfort; Who comforteth us in all our tribulation, that we may be able to comfort them which are in any trouble, by the comfort wherewith we ourselves are comforted of God.

II Corinthians 1:3, 4

Thou preparest a
table before me
in the presence
of mine enemies...

THE VICTORIOUS LIFE

But thanks be to God, which
giveth us the victory through
our Lord Jesus Christ.

I Corinthians 15:57

For whatsoever is born of God
overcometh the world: and this
is the victory that overcometh
the world, even our faith.

I John 5:4

Though an host should encamp
against me, my heart shall not
fear: though war should rise
against me, in this will I be
confident.

Psalm 27:3

And now shall mine head be
lifted up above mine enemies
round about me: therefore will
I offer in his tabernacle sacrifices
of joy; I will sing, yea, I will
sing praises unto the Lord.

Psalm 27:6

...thou anointest my head with oil...

GLADNESS

Serve the Lord with gladness:
come before his presence with
singing.

Psalm 100:2

Thou hast turned for me my
mourning into dancing: thou
hast put off my sackcloth, and
girded me with gladness; To the
end that my glory may sing
praise to thee, and not be
silent. O Lord my God, I will
give thanks unto thee for ever.

Psalm 30:11, 12

Light is sown for the righteous,
and gladness for the upright in
heart.

Psalm 97:11

I was glad when they said unto
me, Let us go into the house of
the Lord.

Psalm 122:1

This is the day which the Lord
hath made; we will rejoice and
be glad in it.

Psalm 118:24

Thou hast put gladness in my
heart ...

Psalm 4:7

...my cup runneth over.

THE JOYFUL LIFE

Rejoice in the Lord alway: and again I say, Rejoice.

Philippians 4:4

Thou wilt shew me the path of life: in thy presence is fulness of joy; at thy right hand there are pleasures for evermore.

Psalm 16:11

The blessing of the Lord, it maketh rich, and he addeth no sorrow with it.

Proverbs 10:22

.... ask, and ye shall receive, that your joy may be full.

John 16:24

For the kingdom of God is not meat and drink; but righteousness, and peace, and joy in the Holy Ghost.

Romans 14:17

... the fruit of the Spirit is ... joy.

Galatians 5:22

Surely goodness and mercy
shall follow me all the
days of my life…

THE GOOD LIFE

The Lord is the portion of mine inheritance and of my cup: thou maintainest my lot. The lines are fallen unto me in pleasant places; yea, I have a goodly heritage.

Psalm 16:5, 6

Every good gift and every perfect gift is from above, and cometh down from the Father of lights, with whom is no variableness, neither shadow of turning.

James 1:17

In this was manifested the love of God toward us, because that God sent his only begotten Son into the world, that we might live through him.

I John 4:9

O taste and see that the Lord is good: blessed is the man that trusteth in him.

Psalm 34:8

Being confident of this very thing, that he which hath begun a good work in you will perform it until the day of Jesus Christ: . . .

Philippians 1:6

For God who commanded the light to shine out of darkness, hath shined in our hearts, to give the light of the knowledge of the glory of God in the face of Jesus Christ.

II Corinthians 4:6

...and I will dwell in the house of the LORD for ever.

ETERNAL LIFE

I am the resurrection, and the life: he that believeth in me, though he were dead, yet shall he live: And whosoever liveth and believeth in me shall never die.

John 11:25, 26

Verily, verily, I say unto you, He that heareth my word, and believeth on him that sent me, hath everlasting life, and shall not come into condemnation; but is passed from death unto life.

John 5:24

For God so loved the world, that he gave his only begotten Son, that whosoever believeth in him should not perish, but have everlasting life.

John 3:16

In my Father's house are many mansions: if it were not so, I would have told you. I go to prepare a place for you. And if I go and prepare a place for you, I will come again, and receive you unto myself; that where I am, there ye may be also.

John 14:2, 3

Now unto him that is able to keep you from falling, and to present you faultless before the presence of his glory with exceeding joy, To the only wise God our Saviour, be glory and majesty, dominion and power, both now and ever. Amen.

Jude 24, 25